50 Thai Dishes

By: Kelly Johnson

Table of Contents

- Pad Thai
- Green Curry with Chicken
- Tom Yum Soup
- Massaman Curry
- Som Tum (Green Papaya Salad)
- Panang Curry with Beef
- Pad See Ew
- Tom Kha Gai (Coconut Soup with Chicken)
- Thai Basil Chicken (Gai Pad Krapow)
- Red Curry with Duck
- Pad Kra Pao with Tofu
- Thai Fried Rice
- Moo Pad Krapow (Pork with Basil)
- Larb Gai (Chicken Salad)
- Thai Fish Cakes (Tod Mun Pla)
- Thai Style Grilled Beef Salad (Nam Tok)
- Thai Spring Rolls (Po Pia Tod)
- Green Curry with Tofu
- Thai BBQ Chicken (Gai Yang)
- Massaman Curry with Lamb
- Thai Coconut Noodles (Khao Soi)
- Stir-Fried Morning Glory (Pad Pak Boong)
- Thai Satay Skewers with Peanut Sauce
- Thai Red Curry with Vegetables
- Khao Pad Sapparot (Pineapple Fried Rice)
- Thai Style Omelette (Khai Jiao)
- Thai Crab Cakes with Sweet Chili Sauce
- Stir-Fried Lemongrass Beef
- Thai Banana Fritters
- Thai Grilled Fish (Pla Pao)
- Pad Kee Mao (Drunken Noodles)
- Thai Green Mango Salad
- Pad Woon Sen (Stir-Fried Glass Noodles)
- Thai Yellow Curry with Chicken
- Thai Chicken Wings with Sweet Chili Sauce

- Thai Seafood Salad (Yum Talay)
- Thai Steamed Fish with Lime and Chili
- Thai Style Prawn Curry
- Thai Mango Sticky Rice
- Thai Beef Curry
- Thai Spicy Pork Soup (Gaeng Om)
- Thai-Style Prawn Cakes
- Thai Sweet and Sour Pork
- Stir-Fried Thai Noodles with Crab
- Thai Coconut Ice Cream
- Spicy Thai Eggplant Stir-Fry
- Thai Stir-Fried Squid with Garlic and Pepper
- Thai Rice Noodles with Grilled Pork
- Thai Pumpkin Curry
- Thai Ginger Chicken Stir-Fry

Pad Thai

Ingredients:

- 8 oz rice noodles
- 2 tablespoons vegetable oil
- 1/2 pound shrimp, peeled and deveined (or chicken, tofu, or vegetables)
- 2 eggs, lightly beaten
- 1 cup bean sprouts
- 1/2 cup green onions, chopped
- 1/4 cup peanuts, crushed
- 2 tablespoons tamarind paste
- 2 tablespoons fish sauce
- 1 tablespoon sugar
- 1 tablespoon lime juice
- 1/2 teaspoon chili flakes (optional)
- Fresh cilantro, for garnish

Instructions:

1. Cook rice noodles according to package instructions, then drain and set aside.
2. In a large wok or skillet, heat oil over medium heat. Add shrimp (or protein of choice) and cook until pink and cooked through. Remove from the pan and set aside.
3. In the same pan, scramble the eggs until cooked through, then push to one side.
4. Add the cooked noodles, tamarind paste, fish sauce, sugar, and lime juice to the pan. Toss to coat the noodles.
5. Add the shrimp, bean sprouts, green onions, and chili flakes (if using). Toss everything together until well combined and heated through.
6. Serve with crushed peanuts and fresh cilantro on top.

Green Curry with Chicken

Ingredients:

- 1 tablespoon vegetable oil
- 1 pound chicken breast, thinly sliced
- 1 can (14 oz) coconut milk
- 2-3 tablespoons green curry paste
- 1 tablespoon fish sauce
- 1 tablespoon brown sugar
- 1/2 cup chicken broth
- 1 red bell pepper, sliced
- 1 zucchini, sliced
- 1/2 cup bamboo shoots (optional)
- Fresh basil and cilantro, for garnish
- Jasmine rice, for serving

Instructions:

1. In a large pot, heat the vegetable oil over medium heat. Add the chicken and cook until browned.
2. Stir in the green curry paste and cook for another minute until fragrant.
3. Pour in the coconut milk, fish sauce, brown sugar, and chicken broth. Stir to combine.
4. Add the bell pepper, zucchini, and bamboo shoots (if using). Bring the curry to a simmer and cook for 10-15 minutes until the vegetables are tender.
5. Serve over jasmine rice and garnish with fresh basil and cilantro.

Tom Yum Soup

Ingredients:

- 4 cups chicken broth
- 1 stalk lemongrass, cut into 3-inch pieces and smashed
- 4-5 kaffir lime leaves, torn into pieces
- 3-4 Thai bird's eye chilies, smashed (adjust to desired spice level)
- 8 oz mushrooms, sliced
- 1/2 pound shrimp, peeled and deveined
- 2-3 tablespoons fish sauce
- 1-2 tablespoons lime juice
- 1 tablespoon sugar
- Fresh cilantro, for garnish

Instructions:

1. In a large pot, bring the chicken broth to a boil. Add the lemongrass, lime leaves, and chilies. Let it simmer for 5-10 minutes to infuse the flavors.
2. Add the mushrooms and shrimp to the pot and cook for 3-4 minutes, until the shrimp turns pink.
3. Stir in the fish sauce, lime juice, and sugar. Taste and adjust the seasoning if needed.
4. Serve the soup hot, garnished with fresh cilantro.

Massaman Curry

Ingredients:

- 1 tablespoon vegetable oil
- 1 pound beef stew meat, cut into chunks
- 1 onion, chopped
- 1 can (14 oz) coconut milk
- 2 tablespoons Massaman curry paste
- 1 tablespoon fish sauce
- 1 tablespoon brown sugar
- 1/2 cup potatoes, peeled and cubed
- 1/2 cup carrots, sliced
- 1/4 cup roasted peanuts
- Fresh cilantro, for garnish
- Jasmine rice, for serving

Instructions:

1. In a large pot, heat the oil over medium heat. Add the beef and brown it on all sides.
2. Add the onion and cook until softened.
3. Stir in the Massaman curry paste and cook for another minute.
4. Pour in the coconut milk, fish sauce, and brown sugar. Stir well.
5. Add the potatoes and carrots, and bring to a simmer. Cook for 30-40 minutes, until the beef is tender and the vegetables are cooked through.
6. Stir in the roasted peanuts and garnish with fresh cilantro.
7. Serve over jasmine rice.

Som Tum (Green Papaya Salad)

Ingredients:

- 2 cups shredded green papaya
- 1/2 cup shredded carrots
- 1/4 cup cherry tomatoes, halved
- 1/4 cup long green beans, cut into 2-inch pieces
- 2 tablespoons fish sauce
- 1 tablespoon lime juice
- 1 tablespoon sugar
- 1-2 Thai bird's eye chilies, smashed (adjust to desired spice level)
- 1 tablespoon crushed peanuts
- Fresh cilantro, for garnish

Instructions:

1. In a large bowl, combine the shredded papaya, carrots, cherry tomatoes, and green beans.
2. In a mortar and pestle or small bowl, crush the chilies with the sugar until fragrant.
3. Add the fish sauce and lime juice to the mixture, stirring to combine.
4. Toss the dressing with the papaya salad, then garnish with crushed peanuts and cilantro.

Panang Curry with Beef

Ingredients:

- 1 tablespoon vegetable oil
- 1 pound beef (sirloin or flank), thinly sliced
- 1 can (14 oz) coconut milk
- 2 tablespoons Panang curry paste
- 1 tablespoon fish sauce
- 1 tablespoon brown sugar
- 1/2 cup bell peppers, sliced
- 1/4 cup chopped basil leaves
- Jasmine rice, for serving

Instructions:

1. In a large skillet, heat oil over medium heat. Add the beef and cook until browned.
2. Stir in the Panang curry paste and cook for another minute.
3. Add the coconut milk, fish sauce, and brown sugar. Stir well and bring to a simmer.
4. Add the bell peppers and cook for 5-10 minutes, until the sauce thickens.
5. Stir in the fresh basil leaves.
6. Serve with jasmine rice.

Pad See Ew

Ingredients:

- 8 oz wide rice noodles
- 2 tablespoons vegetable oil
- 1/2 pound chicken breast, sliced thinly
- 1/2 cup Chinese broccoli, chopped
- 2 eggs, lightly beaten
- 2 tablespoons soy sauce
- 1 tablespoon dark soy sauce
- 1 tablespoon oyster sauce
- 1 teaspoon sugar

Instructions:

1. Cook the rice noodles according to the package instructions, then drain and set aside.
2. Heat oil in a large skillet or wok over medium-high heat. Add the chicken and cook until browned.
3. Add the Chinese broccoli and stir-fry for a couple of minutes.
4. Push everything to the side and scramble the eggs on the other side of the pan.
5. Add the noodles and sauces (soy sauce, dark soy sauce, oyster sauce, and sugar) and toss everything together.
6. Cook for an additional 2-3 minutes until the noodles are well-coated and heated through.

Tom Kha Gai (Coconut Soup with Chicken)

Ingredients:

- 1 tablespoon vegetable oil
- 1 pound chicken breast, thinly sliced
- 4 cups coconut milk
- 1 stalk lemongrass, cut into 3-inch pieces and smashed
- 4-5 kaffir lime leaves, torn into pieces
- 3-4 Thai bird's eye chilies, smashed
- 1/2 cup mushrooms, sliced
- 2 tablespoons fish sauce
- 2 tablespoons lime juice
- Fresh cilantro, for garnish

Instructions:

1. In a pot, heat oil over medium heat. Add the chicken and cook until browned.
2. Add the coconut milk, lemongrass, lime leaves, and chilies. Bring to a simmer and cook for 10 minutes.
3. Add the mushrooms and cook for another 5 minutes.
4. Stir in the fish sauce and lime juice.
5. Serve the soup hot, garnished with fresh cilantro.

Thai Basil Chicken (Gai Pad Krapow)

Ingredients:

- 1 tablespoon vegetable oil
- 1 pound chicken breast, minced
- 4 cloves garlic, minced
- 2-3 Thai bird's eye chilies, smashed (adjust to desired spice level)
- 1 onion, chopped
- 1/2 cup bell pepper, sliced
- 2 tablespoons fish sauce
- 1 tablespoon soy sauce
- 1 tablespoon oyster sauce
- 1 teaspoon sugar
- 1 cup Thai basil leaves
- Jasmine rice, for serving

Instructions:

1. Heat oil in a large skillet or wok over medium-high heat. Add the garlic, chilies, and onion, cooking until fragrant.
2. Add the chicken and cook until browned, breaking it up into smaller pieces.
3. Stir in the bell peppers, fish sauce, soy sauce, oyster sauce, and sugar. Cook for a few minutes until the vegetables are tender.
4. Add the Thai basil leaves and toss until the basil wilts.
5. Serve over jasmine rice.

Red Curry with Duck

Ingredients:

- 1 tablespoon vegetable oil
- 1 pound duck breast, sliced
- 1 can (14 oz) coconut milk
- 2-3 tablespoons red curry paste
- 1 tablespoon fish sauce
- 1 tablespoon brown sugar
- 1/2 cup bell peppers, sliced
- 1/2 cup bamboo shoots
- 1/2 cup Thai basil leaves
- 1 tablespoon lime juice
- Jasmine rice, for serving

Instructions:

1. Heat oil in a large skillet over medium heat. Add the duck slices and cook until browned and crispy.
2. Stir in the red curry paste and cook for another minute.
3. Pour in the coconut milk, fish sauce, and brown sugar. Stir to combine and bring to a simmer.
4. Add the bell peppers and bamboo shoots, cooking for about 5 minutes.
5. Stir in the lime juice and Thai basil leaves.
6. Serve over jasmine rice.

Pad Kra Pao with Tofu

Ingredients:

- 1 tablespoon vegetable oil
- 1 block firm tofu, pressed and cubed
- 4 cloves garlic, minced
- 2-3 Thai bird's eye chilies, smashed (adjust to desired spice level)
- 1/2 cup bell pepper, sliced
- 1 tablespoon soy sauce
- 1 tablespoon oyster sauce
- 1 teaspoon sugar
- 1 cup Thai basil leaves
- Jasmine rice, for serving

Instructions:

1. Heat oil in a wok or large skillet over medium-high heat. Add the tofu cubes and cook until crispy and golden brown. Remove from the pan and set aside.
2. In the same pan, add the garlic and chilies, cooking until fragrant.
3. Add the bell peppers and cook for a few minutes until softened.
4. Stir in the soy sauce, oyster sauce, and sugar.
5. Add the tofu back to the pan and toss everything together. Stir in the Thai basil leaves and cook until they wilt.
6. Serve over jasmine rice.

Thai Fried Rice

Ingredients:

- 2 cups cooked jasmine rice (preferably day-old)
- 1 tablespoon vegetable oil
- 2 eggs, beaten
- 1/2 cup cooked chicken, shrimp, or pork (optional)
- 2 cloves garlic, minced
- 1/4 cup frozen peas and carrots
- 2 tablespoons fish sauce
- 1 tablespoon soy sauce
- 1 teaspoon sugar
- 1/4 cup green onions, chopped
- 1/4 cup cilantro, chopped
- Lime wedges, for serving

Instructions:

1. Heat oil in a large skillet or wok over medium heat. Add the eggs and scramble until cooked through. Remove from the pan and set aside.
2. In the same pan, add the garlic and cook for 1 minute until fragrant.
3. Add the peas, carrots, and cooked chicken (or other protein) and stir-fry for a few minutes.
4. Stir in the rice, breaking up any clumps. Add the fish sauce, soy sauce, and sugar, mixing well.
5. Add the scrambled eggs back to the pan and toss everything together.
6. Garnish with green onions and cilantro. Serve with lime wedges.

Moo Pad Krapow (Pork with Basil)

Ingredients:

- 1 tablespoon vegetable oil
- 1 pound ground pork
- 4 cloves garlic, minced
- 2-3 Thai bird's eye chilies, smashed (adjust to desired spice level)
- 1/2 onion, chopped
- 1 tablespoon fish sauce
- 1 tablespoon soy sauce
- 1 teaspoon sugar
- 1 cup Thai basil leaves
- Jasmine rice, for serving

Instructions:

1. Heat oil in a skillet over medium-high heat. Add the garlic, chilies, and onion, cooking until fragrant.
2. Add the ground pork and cook until browned and cooked through, breaking it up into smaller pieces.
3. Stir in the fish sauce, soy sauce, and sugar. Cook for a few more minutes until the sauce is well absorbed.
4. Add the basil leaves and stir until wilted.
5. Serve over jasmine rice.

Larb Gai (Chicken Salad)

Ingredients:

- 1 pound ground chicken
- 1 tablespoon vegetable oil
- 1/4 cup red onion, finely sliced
- 1 tablespoon fish sauce
- 1 tablespoon lime juice
- 1 teaspoon sugar
- 1/4 cup fresh mint, chopped
- 1/4 cup cilantro, chopped
- 2 tablespoons toasted rice powder (optional)
- 1 Thai bird's eye chili, minced (optional)

Instructions:

1. Heat oil in a skillet over medium heat. Add the ground chicken and cook until browned, breaking it into small pieces.
2. In a bowl, combine the fish sauce, lime juice, and sugar.
3. Add the cooked chicken, onion, mint, cilantro, and toasted rice powder (if using). Toss everything together.
4. Garnish with additional mint and cilantro. Serve as a salad or with sticky rice.

Thai Fish Cakes (Tod Mun Pla)

Ingredients:

- 1/2 pound white fish fillets (like tilapia), minced
- 1 tablespoon red curry paste
- 1 tablespoon fish sauce
- 1 tablespoon lime juice
- 1 egg, beaten
- 1/4 cup green beans, chopped
- 1/4 cup Thai basil leaves, chopped
- 1/4 cup breadcrumbs
- Vegetable oil, for frying
- Cucumber and chili dipping sauce, for serving

Instructions:

1. In a bowl, combine the fish, curry paste, fish sauce, lime juice, egg, green beans, and basil. Mix well.
2. Form the mixture into small patties.
3. Heat oil in a frying pan over medium heat. Fry the patties in batches until golden and cooked through.
4. Serve with a cucumber and chili dipping sauce.

Thai Style Grilled Beef Salad (Nam Tok)

Ingredients:

- 1 pound flank steak
- 1 tablespoon vegetable oil
- 1 tablespoon soy sauce
- 1 tablespoon fish sauce
- 1 tablespoon lime juice
- 1 teaspoon sugar
- 1/2 red onion, thinly sliced
- 1/2 cucumber, thinly sliced
- 1/4 cup cilantro, chopped
- 1/4 cup mint leaves, chopped
- 1 Thai bird's eye chili, minced (optional)

Instructions:

1. Preheat the grill or a grill pan over medium-high heat. Rub the steak with oil and grill for 3-5 minutes per side, or to your desired doneness.
2. Let the steak rest for 5 minutes, then slice thinly against the grain.
3. In a bowl, combine the soy sauce, fish sauce, lime juice, and sugar. Toss the steak slices in the dressing.
4. Add the onion, cucumber, cilantro, mint, and chili (if using), and toss everything together.
5. Serve immediately.

Thai Spring Rolls (Po Pia Tod)

Ingredients:

- 8-10 rice paper wrappers
- 1/2 pound shrimp, peeled and deveined (optional)
- 1/2 cup cooked vermicelli noodles
- 1 cup shredded lettuce
- 1/2 cup shredded carrots
- 1/4 cup fresh cilantro leaves
- 1/4 cup fresh mint leaves
- 1/4 cup Thai basil leaves
- 1/2 cucumber, julienned
- 1 tablespoon hoisin sauce (for dipping)
- 1 tablespoon peanut butter (for dipping)

Instructions:

1. Soak the rice paper wrappers in warm water until soft, about 15-20 seconds.
2. Place the wrapper on a flat surface. Add a small amount of shrimp (optional), vermicelli noodles, lettuce, carrots, cucumber, and herbs in the center of the wrapper.
3. Fold the sides of the wrapper over the filling and roll tightly.
4. Mix hoisin sauce and peanut butter to make a dipping sauce.
5. Serve the spring rolls with the dipping sauce.

Green Curry with Tofu

Ingredients:

- 1 tablespoon vegetable oil
- 1/2 cup green curry paste
- 1 can (14 oz) coconut milk
- 1/2 cup vegetable broth
- 1 block firm tofu, cubed
- 1/2 cup bamboo shoots
- 1/2 cup bell peppers, sliced
- 1/2 cup zucchini, sliced
- 1/4 cup Thai basil leaves
- 1 tablespoon soy sauce
- 1 tablespoon lime juice
- Jasmine rice, for serving

Instructions:

1. Heat oil in a large pot over medium heat. Add the green curry paste and cook for 1 minute until fragrant.
2. Add the coconut milk and vegetable broth, stirring to combine.
3. Add the tofu, bamboo shoots, bell peppers, and zucchini. Simmer for 10-15 minutes until vegetables are tender.
4. Stir in soy sauce, lime juice, and Thai basil leaves.
5. Serve with jasmine rice.

Thai BBQ Chicken (Gai Yang)

Ingredients:

- 4 chicken thighs, bone-in and skin-on
- 2 tablespoons vegetable oil
- 3 cloves garlic, minced
- 2 tablespoons soy sauce
- 2 tablespoons fish sauce
- 1 tablespoon lime juice
- 1 tablespoon brown sugar
- 1/2 teaspoon turmeric powder
- 1/4 teaspoon white pepper

Instructions:

1. In a bowl, combine garlic, soy sauce, fish sauce, lime juice, brown sugar, turmeric, and white pepper.
2. Marinate the chicken thighs in the mixture for at least 1 hour (or overnight for more flavor).
3. Heat a grill or grill pan over medium-high heat. Cook the chicken thighs for 6-7 minutes per side, until fully cooked and golden brown.
4. Serve with steamed rice and Thai dipping sauce.

Massaman Curry with Lamb

Ingredients:

- 1 tablespoon vegetable oil
- 1 pound lamb, cut into chunks
- 1/2 onion, chopped
- 2 tablespoons Massaman curry paste
- 1 can (14 oz) coconut milk
- 1/2 cup beef broth
- 2 potatoes, peeled and cubed
- 1/2 cup roasted peanuts, chopped
- 1 tablespoon fish sauce
- 1 tablespoon brown sugar
- Jasmine rice, for serving

Instructions:

1. Heat oil in a large pot over medium-high heat. Brown the lamb chunks on all sides, then remove and set aside.
2. Add the onions to the pot and cook until softened. Stir in the Massaman curry paste and cook for 1 minute.
3. Add the coconut milk, beef broth, and potatoes. Bring to a boil and then reduce to a simmer. Cook for 20-25 minutes until the lamb is tender.
4. Stir in the peanuts, fish sauce, and brown sugar. Cook for an additional 5 minutes.
5. Serve with jasmine rice.

Thai Coconut Noodles (Khao Soi)

Ingredients:

- 1 tablespoon vegetable oil
- 1/2 onion, chopped
- 2 cloves garlic, minced
- 1 tablespoon yellow curry paste
- 1 can (14 oz) coconut milk
- 2 cups vegetable broth
- 1 tablespoon soy sauce
- 1 tablespoon lime juice
- 1 teaspoon sugar
- 8 oz egg noodles, cooked
- 1/2 cup crispy fried noodles
- Fresh cilantro, chopped, for garnish
- Lime wedges, for serving

Instructions:

1. Heat oil in a large pot over medium heat. Add the onion and garlic, cooking until softened.
2. Stir in the yellow curry paste and cook for 1 minute.
3. Add the coconut milk, vegetable broth, soy sauce, lime juice, and sugar. Bring to a boil, then reduce the heat to simmer for 10-15 minutes.
4. Divide the cooked noodles into bowls and pour the soup over the noodles.
5. Top with crispy fried noodles, fresh cilantro, and lime wedges. Serve hot.

Stir-Fried Morning Glory (Pad Pak Boong)

Ingredients:

- 2 tablespoons vegetable oil
- 2 cloves garlic, minced
- 1-2 Thai bird's eye chilies, smashed (optional)
- 1 pound morning glory (water spinach), washed and chopped
- 1 tablespoon soy sauce
- 1 tablespoon oyster sauce
- 1 teaspoon sugar
- 1/4 cup water

Instructions:

1. Heat oil in a wok over high heat. Add the garlic and chilies, cooking until fragrant.
2. Add the morning glory and stir-fry for a few minutes until wilted.
3. Stir in the soy sauce, oyster sauce, and sugar. Add water and cook for another 1-2 minutes until the vegetables are tender.
4. Serve as a side dish.

Thai Satay Skewers with Peanut Sauce

Ingredients:

- 1 pound chicken breast, thinly sliced into strips
- 1/4 cup coconut milk
- 1 tablespoon soy sauce
- 1 tablespoon curry powder
- 1 tablespoon lime juice
- 1 tablespoon brown sugar
- 1/4 teaspoon turmeric powder
- 1 tablespoon vegetable oil
- Wooden skewers, soaked in water

Peanut Sauce:

- 1/4 cup peanut butter
- 1 tablespoon soy sauce
- 1 tablespoon lime juice
- 1 tablespoon brown sugar
- 1/4 cup coconut milk
- 1/2 teaspoon chili paste (optional)

Instructions:

1. In a bowl, mix coconut milk, soy sauce, curry powder, lime juice, brown sugar, and turmeric powder. Add the chicken strips and marinate for at least 30 minutes.
2. Thread the marinated chicken onto the skewers.
3. Heat oil in a grill pan over medium-high heat. Grill the skewers for 3-4 minutes on each side until cooked through.
4. For the peanut sauce, whisk together peanut butter, soy sauce, lime juice, brown sugar, coconut milk, and chili paste in a bowl.
5. Serve the chicken skewers with the peanut sauce.

Thai Red Curry with Vegetables

Ingredients:

- 1 tablespoon vegetable oil
- 1 tablespoon red curry paste
- 1 can (14 oz) coconut milk
- 1/2 cup vegetable broth
- 1/2 cup carrots, sliced
- 1/2 cup bell peppers, sliced
- 1/2 cup zucchini, sliced
- 1/2 cup baby corn
- 1/4 cup Thai basil leaves
- 1 tablespoon soy sauce
- 1 tablespoon lime juice
- Jasmine rice, for serving

Instructions:

1. Heat oil in a large pot over medium heat. Add the red curry paste and cook for 1 minute.
2. Pour in the coconut milk and vegetable broth. Stir to combine.
3. Add the carrots, bell peppers, zucchini, and baby corn. Simmer for 10-15 minutes until the vegetables are tender.
4. Stir in soy sauce, lime juice, and Thai basil leaves.
5. Serve with jasmine rice.

Khao Pad Sapparot (Pineapple Fried Rice)

Ingredients:

- 2 tablespoons vegetable oil
- 2 cloves garlic, minced
- 1/2 onion, chopped
- 1/2 cup cooked chicken or shrimp (optional)
- 2 cups cooked jasmine rice (preferably day-old)
- 1/2 cup pineapple chunks
- 1/4 cup peas and carrots
- 1 tablespoon soy sauce
- 1 tablespoon fish sauce
- 1 teaspoon curry powder
- 1/4 cup roasted cashews
- 1/4 cup green onions, chopped
- Lime wedges, for serving

Instructions:

1. Heat oil in a large wok over medium-high heat. Add garlic and onion, cooking until fragrant.
2. Stir in chicken or shrimp (if using), pineapple, peas, and carrots. Cook for a few minutes until heated through.
3. Add the rice, breaking up any clumps. Stir in soy sauce, fish sauce, and curry powder.
4. Cook for another 3-4 minutes until everything is well combined.
5. Stir in cashews and green onions.
6. Serve with lime wedges.

Thai Style Omelette (Khai Jiao)

Ingredients:

- 3 eggs
- 1 tablespoon fish sauce
- 1/4 teaspoon white pepper
- 1/2 small onion, chopped
- 1/4 cup cilantro, chopped
- 1-2 Thai bird's eye chilies, finely chopped (optional)
- 2 tablespoons vegetable oil

Instructions:

1. Crack the eggs into a bowl and whisk with fish sauce, white pepper, onions, cilantro, and chilies (if using).
2. Heat the oil in a wok or large frying pan over medium-high heat.
3. Pour the egg mixture into the pan and let it cook without stirring for 2-3 minutes, until the bottom is golden and crispy.
4. Flip the omelette and cook for an additional 1-2 minutes until fully cooked.
5. Serve with steamed rice and a side of chili sauce.

Thai Crab Cakes with Sweet Chili Sauce

Ingredients:

- 1/2 pound crab meat, picked through for shells
- 1/4 cup breadcrumbs
- 1/4 cup finely chopped cilantro
- 1/4 cup finely chopped green onions
- 1 egg, beaten
- 1 tablespoon fish sauce
- 1 teaspoon lime juice
- 1 tablespoon red curry paste
- 1 tablespoon vegetable oil
- Sweet chili sauce, for dipping

Instructions:

1. In a large bowl, mix crab meat, breadcrumbs, cilantro, green onions, egg, fish sauce, lime juice, and curry paste.
2. Form the mixture into small patties.
3. Heat vegetable oil in a pan over medium heat. Fry the crab cakes for 3-4 minutes on each side until golden brown.
4. Serve with sweet chili sauce for dipping.

Stir-Fried Lemongrass Beef

Ingredients:

- 1 pound beef (sirloin or flank steak), thinly sliced
- 2 tablespoons vegetable oil
- 2 stalks lemongrass, finely chopped
- 3 cloves garlic, minced
- 1-2 Thai bird's eye chilies, minced (optional)
- 2 tablespoons fish sauce
- 1 tablespoon soy sauce
- 1 tablespoon lime juice
- 1 tablespoon brown sugar
- Fresh cilantro, chopped, for garnish
- Jasmine rice, for serving

Instructions:

1. Heat the oil in a wok over medium-high heat. Add lemongrass, garlic, and chilies (if using), and stir-fry for 1-2 minutes until fragrant.
2. Add the sliced beef to the wok and stir-fry until cooked through, about 3-4 minutes.
3. Stir in fish sauce, soy sauce, lime juice, and brown sugar. Cook for another minute.
4. Garnish with fresh cilantro and serve with jasmine rice.

Thai Banana Fritters

Ingredients:

- 4 ripe bananas, sliced into 1/2-inch pieces
- 1/2 cup rice flour
- 1/4 cup all-purpose flour
- 1/4 teaspoon baking powder
- 1/4 teaspoon salt
- 1 tablespoon sugar
- 1/2 cup coconut milk
- Vegetable oil, for frying
- Powdered sugar (optional)

Instructions:

1. In a bowl, mix the rice flour, all-purpose flour, baking powder, salt, and sugar.
2. Add coconut milk and stir to form a batter.
3. Heat oil in a frying pan over medium heat.
4. Dip banana slices into the batter and fry until golden brown, about 2-3 minutes on each side.
5. Remove from oil and drain on paper towels. Dust with powdered sugar before serving.

Thai Grilled Fish (Pla Pao)

Ingredients:

- 2 whole fish (tilapia, snapper, or any white fish)
- 2 tablespoons vegetable oil
- 3 cloves garlic, minced
- 2 tablespoons fish sauce
- 1 tablespoon lime juice
- 1 tablespoon chopped cilantro
- 1 tablespoon Thai chili paste (optional)
- Banana leaves or aluminum foil for grilling

Instructions:

1. Preheat the grill to medium-high heat.
2. Clean and gut the fish, leaving the head and tail intact. Score the fish on both sides.
3. Mix garlic, fish sauce, lime juice, cilantro, and chili paste (if using) in a small bowl.
4. Rub the mixture over the fish, making sure to coat both the inside and outside.
5. Wrap the fish in banana leaves or foil and grill for 10-12 minutes on each side, until fully cooked.
6. Serve with steamed rice and dipping sauce.

Pad Kee Mao (Drunken Noodles)

Ingredients:

- 8 oz wide rice noodles
- 1 tablespoon vegetable oil
- 3 cloves garlic, minced
- 2 Thai bird's eye chilies, chopped
- 1/2 cup bell peppers, sliced
- 1/2 cup Thai basil leaves
- 1 tablespoon soy sauce
- 1 tablespoon fish sauce
- 1 tablespoon oyster sauce
- 1 teaspoon sugar
- 1/4 cup water

Instructions:

1. Cook the rice noodles according to package directions. Drain and set aside.
2. Heat oil in a wok over medium-high heat. Add garlic and chilies, cooking until fragrant.
3. Add bell peppers and stir-fry for 2 minutes until slightly tender.
4. Stir in soy sauce, fish sauce, oyster sauce, and sugar.
5. Add the cooked noodles and water, stir-frying until the noodles are coated with sauce.
6. Stir in basil leaves and cook for another minute.
7. Serve hot with additional basil leaves for garnish.

Thai Green Mango Salad

Ingredients:

- 2 green mangoes, peeled and julienned
- 1/2 cup shredded carrots
- 1/4 cup fresh cilantro, chopped
- 1/4 cup roasted peanuts, chopped
- 1-2 Thai bird's eye chilies, chopped (optional)
- 2 tablespoons fish sauce
- 1 tablespoon lime juice
- 1 tablespoon sugar

Instructions:

1. In a large bowl, combine the julienned mango, shredded carrots, cilantro, and peanuts.
2. In a small bowl, whisk together fish sauce, lime juice, sugar, and chilies (if using).
3. Pour the dressing over the salad and toss to combine.
4. Serve immediately as a refreshing side dish or appetizer.

Pad Woon Sen (Stir-Fried Glass Noodles)

Ingredients:

- 8 oz glass noodles (mung bean noodles)
- 2 tablespoons vegetable oil
- 2 cloves garlic, minced
- 1/2 cup sliced mushrooms
- 1/2 cup carrots, julienned
- 1/2 cup bell peppers, sliced
- 1/2 cup baby corn
- 2 tablespoons soy sauce
- 1 tablespoon fish sauce
- 1 tablespoon oyster sauce
- 1/2 teaspoon white pepper
- 1/4 cup green onions, chopped

Instructions:

1. Soak the glass noodles in warm water for 20 minutes, then drain.
2. Heat oil in a wok over medium-high heat. Add garlic and stir-fry for 1 minute.
3. Add mushrooms, carrots, bell peppers, and baby corn. Stir-fry for 3-4 minutes.
4. Stir in soy sauce, fish sauce, oyster sauce, and white pepper.
5. Add the soaked noodles and stir-fry for another 2-3 minutes until heated through.
6. Garnish with green onions and serve.

Thai Yellow Curry with Chicken

Ingredients:

- 1 tablespoon vegetable oil
- 1 pound chicken breast, sliced
- 2 tablespoons yellow curry paste
- 1 can (14 oz) coconut milk
- 1/2 cup chicken broth
- 1/2 cup potatoes, cubed
- 1/2 cup carrots, sliced
- 1/4 cup peas
- 1 tablespoon fish sauce
- 1 tablespoon brown sugar
- 1 tablespoon lime juice
- Jasmine rice, for serving

Instructions:

1. Heat oil in a pot over medium heat. Add chicken breast and cook until browned, about 5 minutes.
2. Stir in yellow curry paste and cook for 1 minute.
3. Add coconut milk, chicken broth, potatoes, and carrots. Bring to a boil, then reduce to a simmer. Cook for 20-25 minutes until the vegetables are tender.
4. Stir in peas, fish sauce, brown sugar, and lime juice.
5. Serve with jasmine rice.

Thai Chicken Wings with Sweet Chili Sauce

Ingredients:

- 12 chicken wings, split and tips removed
- 2 tablespoons vegetable oil
- 2 cloves garlic, minced
- 1/4 cup soy sauce
- 2 tablespoons fish sauce
- 1 tablespoon brown sugar
- 2 tablespoons lime juice
- 1/4 cup sweet chili sauce
- 1 tablespoon chopped cilantro (for garnish)

Instructions:

1. Preheat your oven to 400°F (200°C).
2. In a bowl, mix the soy sauce, fish sauce, brown sugar, lime juice, and sweet chili sauce.
3. Place the chicken wings on a baking sheet lined with parchment paper. Brush the wings with the sauce mixture.
4. Bake for 30-35 minutes, flipping halfway through, until the wings are golden brown and crispy.
5. Garnish with chopped cilantro and serve with extra sweet chili sauce on the side.

Thai Seafood Salad (Yum Talay)

Ingredients:

- 1/2 pound shrimp, peeled and deveined
- 1/2 pound squid, cleaned and sliced into rings
- 1/2 pound mussels, cleaned
- 1 cucumber, sliced thinly
- 1/2 red onion, thinly sliced
- 1/4 cup fresh cilantro, chopped
- 1-2 Thai bird's eye chilies, chopped (optional)
- 2 tablespoons fish sauce
- 1 tablespoon lime juice
- 1 tablespoon sugar
- 1/4 cup chopped mint leaves

Instructions:

1. Cook the shrimp, squid, and mussels in boiling water for 2-3 minutes or until fully cooked. Drain and let cool.
2. In a large bowl, combine the seafood, cucumber, red onion, cilantro, chilies (if using), and mint.
3. In a small bowl, whisk together fish sauce, lime juice, and sugar until the sugar dissolves.
4. Pour the dressing over the seafood and toss well to combine.
5. Serve immediately as a refreshing appetizer or main dish.

Thai Steamed Fish with Lime and Chili

Ingredients:

- 1 whole fish (tilapia, snapper, or any white fish), cleaned and gutted
- 2 stalks lemongrass, smashed
- 2-3 Thai bird's eye chilies, smashed
- 3 cloves garlic, smashed
- 1/4 cup fish sauce
- 2 tablespoons lime juice
- 1 tablespoon sugar
- 2 sprigs cilantro, chopped (for garnish)

Instructions:

1. Steam the fish in a steamer basket or a large pot with a lid for 10-15 minutes, depending on the size of the fish, until fully cooked.
2. In a small saucepan, combine the lemongrass, chilies, garlic, fish sauce, lime juice, and sugar. Bring to a simmer and cook for 2-3 minutes.
3. Pour the sauce over the steamed fish.
4. Garnish with chopped cilantro and serve immediately.

Thai Style Prawn Curry

Ingredients:

- 1 pound prawns, peeled and deveined
- 2 tablespoons vegetable oil
- 2 tablespoons red curry paste
- 1 can (14 oz) coconut milk
- 1/2 cup chicken broth
- 1 tablespoon fish sauce
- 1 tablespoon lime juice
- 1/2 teaspoon sugar
- 1/4 cup Thai basil leaves
- 1/4 cup cilantro, chopped

Instructions:

1. Heat the oil in a pan over medium heat and sauté the curry paste for 1-2 minutes until fragrant.
2. Add the coconut milk and chicken broth to the pan. Bring to a simmer.
3. Stir in fish sauce, lime juice, and sugar.
4. Add the prawns and cook for 3-4 minutes until they turn pink.
5. Stir in the Thai basil leaves and cilantro just before serving.
6. Serve the curry hot with jasmine rice.

Thai Mango Sticky Rice

Ingredients:

- 1 cup sticky rice (glutinous rice)
- 1 can (14 oz) coconut milk
- 1/4 cup sugar
- 1/4 teaspoon salt
- 2 ripe mangoes, peeled and sliced
- Sesame seeds or mung beans for garnish (optional)

Instructions:

1. Rinse the sticky rice under cold water until the water runs clear. Soak the rice for at least 1 hour.
2. Steam the rice for 30-40 minutes, or until tender.
3. In a small saucepan, heat the coconut milk, sugar, and salt over low heat until the sugar dissolves.
4. Once the rice is cooked, transfer it to a bowl and pour the coconut milk mixture over it. Stir to combine and let it sit for 10 minutes.
5. Serve the coconut sticky rice with sliced mangoes, garnished with sesame seeds or mung beans if desired.

Thai Beef Curry

Ingredients:

- 1 pound beef, sliced thinly
- 2 tablespoons vegetable oil
- 2 tablespoons green curry paste
- 1 can (14 oz) coconut milk
- 1/2 cup beef broth
- 1/2 cup bamboo shoots, sliced
- 1/2 cup bell peppers, sliced
- 1 tablespoon fish sauce
- 1 tablespoon sugar
- Thai basil leaves for garnish

Instructions:

1. Heat the oil in a large pot over medium heat. Add the green curry paste and cook for 1-2 minutes.
2. Add the beef slices and cook until browned, about 5-6 minutes.
3. Stir in the coconut milk, beef broth, bamboo shoots, and bell peppers.
4. Add fish sauce and sugar. Simmer for 20 minutes, or until the beef is tender.
5. Garnish with fresh Thai basil leaves and serve with rice.

Thai Spicy Pork Soup (Gaeng Om)

Ingredients:

- 1/2 pound pork shoulder, thinly sliced
- 2 tablespoons vegetable oil
- 1 tablespoon red curry paste
- 4 cups pork broth or water
- 2 stalks lemongrass, smashed
- 3 kaffir lime leaves
- 2 Thai bird's eye chilies, chopped
- 1 tablespoon fish sauce
- 1 tablespoon lime juice
- 1/2 cup mushrooms, sliced
- 1/4 cup cilantro, chopped

Instructions:

1. Heat oil in a pot and sauté the curry paste for 1-2 minutes.
2. Add the pork and cook until browned.
3. Add the broth, lemongrass, kaffir lime leaves, chilies, fish sauce, and lime juice. Bring to a boil.
4. Lower the heat and simmer for 20-25 minutes.
5. Add the mushrooms and cook for an additional 5 minutes.
6. Garnish with cilantro and serve with steamed rice.

Thai-Style Prawn Cakes

Ingredients:

- 1/2 pound shrimp, peeled and deveined
- 2 tablespoons red curry paste
- 1/4 cup chopped cilantro
- 2 tablespoons fish sauce
- 1 egg, beaten
- 1/4 cup breadcrumbs
- 2 tablespoons vegetable oil
- Sweet chili sauce for dipping

Instructions:

1. Finely chop the shrimp or pulse them in a food processor until a paste-like consistency forms.
2. In a bowl, mix the shrimp, red curry paste, cilantro, fish sauce, egg, and breadcrumbs.
3. Form the mixture into small patties.
4. Heat the oil in a frying pan over medium heat and fry the prawn cakes for 3-4 minutes on each side, until golden and crispy.
5. Serve with sweet chili sauce for dipping.

Thai Sweet and Sour Pork

Ingredients:

- 1 pound pork tenderloin, cut into cubes
- 2 tablespoons vegetable oil
- 1/2 onion, sliced
- 1/2 red bell pepper, sliced
- 1/2 green bell pepper, sliced
- 1/2 cup pineapple chunks
- 1 tablespoon soy sauce
- 1 tablespoon rice vinegar
- 2 tablespoons ketchup
- 1 tablespoon sugar
- 1 tablespoon fish sauce
- 1 tablespoon lime juice

Instructions:

1. Heat the oil in a wok or large skillet over medium-high heat. Add the pork and cook until browned.
2. Add the onion and bell peppers, stir-frying for 2-3 minutes until slightly tender.
3. Stir in the pineapple chunks, soy sauce, rice vinegar, ketchup, sugar, fish sauce, and lime juice.
4. Cook for an additional 5 minutes until the sauce thickens slightly.
5. Serve hot with steamed rice.

Stir-Fried Thai Noodles with Crab

Ingredients:

- 8 oz rice noodles
- 1 tablespoon vegetable oil
- 2 cloves garlic, minced
- 1/2 pound crab meat (fresh or canned)
- 1 egg, lightly beaten
- 1/4 cup fish sauce
- 1 tablespoon soy sauce
- 1 tablespoon sugar
- 1/2 teaspoon chili flakes (optional)
- 1/2 cup bean sprouts
- 2 green onions, chopped
- Fresh cilantro for garnish
- Lime wedges for serving

Instructions:

1. Cook the rice noodles according to the package instructions, then drain and set aside.
2. In a wok or large skillet, heat the vegetable oil over medium-high heat. Add the garlic and stir-fry for 1 minute until fragrant.
3. Add the crab meat and cook for another 2-3 minutes until heated through.
4. Push the crab to one side of the pan and pour the beaten egg into the other side. Scramble the egg until fully cooked.
5. Add the cooked noodles, fish sauce, soy sauce, sugar, and chili flakes (if using). Toss everything together until well combined.
6. Stir in the bean sprouts and green onions. Continue to cook for 1-2 more minutes.
7. Serve garnished with fresh cilantro and lime wedges on the side.

Thai Coconut Ice Cream

Ingredients:

- 2 cups coconut milk
- 1 cup heavy cream
- 3/4 cup sugar
- 1/2 teaspoon vanilla extract
- Pinch of salt
- 1/4 cup shredded coconut (optional)
- Chopped toasted peanuts or toasted coconut for garnish (optional)

Instructions:

1. In a medium saucepan, combine the coconut milk, heavy cream, sugar, vanilla extract, and a pinch of salt. Heat over medium heat, stirring occasionally, until the sugar has dissolved and the mixture is warm (not boiling).
2. Remove from heat and let the mixture cool to room temperature.
3. If you have an ice cream maker, pour the mixture into the machine and churn according to the manufacturer's instructions.
4. If you don't have an ice cream maker, pour the mixture into a shallow pan, cover, and freeze. Stir every 30 minutes until it reaches a smooth, creamy consistency (this may take about 4 hours).
5. Once the ice cream is ready, scoop it into bowls and garnish with shredded coconut or toasted peanuts, if desired.

Spicy Thai Eggplant Stir-Fry

Ingredients:

- 2 medium eggplants, cut into bite-sized pieces
- 2 tablespoons vegetable oil
- 3 cloves garlic, minced
- 2 Thai bird's eye chilies, chopped (adjust to taste)
- 1 tablespoon fish sauce
- 1 tablespoon soy sauce
- 1 tablespoon sugar
- 1/4 cup water
- 1/4 cup Thai basil leaves
- Lime wedges for serving

Instructions:

1. Heat the vegetable oil in a wok or large pan over medium-high heat. Add the garlic and chilies, stir-frying for 1-2 minutes until fragrant.
2. Add the eggplant pieces and stir-fry for 4-5 minutes until they begin to soften.
3. Stir in the fish sauce, soy sauce, sugar, and water. Cook for another 5-7 minutes until the eggplant is tender and the sauce has thickened slightly.
4. Stir in the Thai basil leaves and cook for another 1 minute.
5. Serve hot with lime wedges on the side.

Thai Stir-Fried Squid with Garlic and Pepper

Ingredients:

- 1 pound squid, cleaned and sliced into rings
- 2 tablespoons vegetable oil
- 3 cloves garlic, minced
- 2 Thai bird's eye chilies, chopped (optional)
- 1 tablespoon fish sauce
- 1 tablespoon soy sauce
- 1/2 teaspoon sugar
- 1/4 cup fresh cilantro, chopped
- 1 tablespoon black pepper (or to taste)

Instructions:

1. Heat the vegetable oil in a wok or large skillet over medium-high heat. Add the garlic and chilies, stir-frying for 1 minute until fragrant.
2. Add the squid and cook for 2-3 minutes until just cooked through.
3. Stir in the fish sauce, soy sauce, and sugar, and cook for another 1-2 minutes.
4. Sprinkle with black pepper and stir in the fresh cilantro.
5. Serve hot with steamed rice.

Thai Rice Noodles with Grilled Pork

Ingredients:

- 8 oz rice noodles
- 1/2 pound pork tenderloin or pork shoulder, thinly sliced
- 1 tablespoon soy sauce
- 1 tablespoon fish sauce
- 1 tablespoon brown sugar
- 2 cloves garlic, minced
- 1 tablespoon vegetable oil
- 1/2 cup chopped cilantro
- 1/4 cup chopped peanuts
- 1 lime, cut into wedges

Instructions:

1. Cook the rice noodles according to the package instructions, then drain and set aside.
2. In a bowl, combine the soy sauce, fish sauce, brown sugar, and minced garlic. Add the sliced pork and marinate for at least 30 minutes.
3. Heat the vegetable oil in a grill pan over medium-high heat. Grill the pork slices for 3-4 minutes on each side until fully cooked.
4. Toss the cooked rice noodles with the grilled pork, cilantro, and chopped peanuts.
5. Serve with lime wedges on the side.

Thai Pumpkin Curry

Ingredients:

- 2 cups pumpkin, cubed
- 1 tablespoon vegetable oil
- 1 onion, chopped
- 2 tablespoons red curry paste
- 1 can (14 oz) coconut milk
- 1/2 cup vegetable broth
- 1 tablespoon fish sauce
- 1 tablespoon brown sugar
- 1/4 cup Thai basil leaves
- 1 red bell pepper, sliced
- 1 tablespoon lime juice

Instructions:

1. Heat the oil in a large pot over medium heat. Add the onion and sauté until soft, about 5 minutes.
2. Stir in the red curry paste and cook for 1-2 minutes.
3. Add the pumpkin, coconut milk, vegetable broth, fish sauce, and brown sugar. Bring to a simmer and cook for 15-20 minutes, until the pumpkin is tender.
4. Stir in the bell pepper and cook for another 5 minutes.
5. Remove from heat and stir in the lime juice and Thai basil leaves.
6. Serve hot with steamed rice.

Thai Ginger Chicken Stir-Fry

Ingredients:

- 1 pound chicken breast, thinly sliced
- 2 tablespoons vegetable oil
- 3 cloves garlic, minced
- 1 tablespoon ginger, grated
- 1 tablespoon soy sauce
- 1 tablespoon fish sauce
- 1/2 tablespoon sugar
- 1/2 cup mushrooms, sliced
- 1/4 cup water
- 1/4 cup green onions, chopped
- 1 tablespoon sesame oil

Instructions:

1. Heat the vegetable oil in a wok or large skillet over medium-high heat. Add the garlic and ginger, stir-frying for 1-2 minutes until fragrant.
2. Add the chicken and cook until browned, about 5 minutes.
3. Stir in the soy sauce, fish sauce, sugar, mushrooms, and water. Cook for another 5-7 minutes until the chicken is cooked through.
4. Drizzle with sesame oil and stir in the green onions.
5. Serve hot with steamed rice.

www.ingramcontent.com/pod-product-compliance
Lightning Source LLC
LaVergne TN
LVHW081505060526
838201LV00056BA/2945